HEART'S
DESIRE

PATSY ODA

HEART'S DESIRE

Blessings —
Patsy Oda

He was everything Patsy ever dreamed of...
except for one important quality.
She sent him away more than once,
but he kept coming back.

WINEPRESS WP PUBLISHING

ACKNOWLEDGMENTS

I thank God for the many
wonderful people he
brought to help me
through the process of
writing this book. I wish I
could name every person
who prayed, advised,
typed, critiqued, and en-
couraged me along the
way, but the list would be
too long.

However, I would like to
at least mention those to
whom I feel especially in-
debted:

Ethel Herr and the "Parts
    of Speech" critique ladies
Pastor Gerald J. Pluimer
    and the San Jose Open
    Bible Church.
Virginia Muir and other
    editors and teachers at
    the Mount Hermon
    Christian Writers Con-
    ferences
Kari Ann Martin, my per-
    sonal Tyndale editor
Walter, my constant, loving
    encourager

With sincere appreciation
for each of you,
Patsy

Scripture quotations are from The
Living Bible unless otherwise noted.

Library of Congress Catalog Card
Number
98-60323
ISBN 1-57921-109-7
Copyright 1998 by
Patsy Oda

02 01 00 99 98
8 7 6 5 4

Lovingly dedicated to
Reverend and Mrs. A. A. Smith
and
Joanne (Smith) Olfert

CONTENTS

ONE

My First Love

Through a delicate bridal veil I gazed at my chosen husband, whom I had so long tried not to love. Could it be that I was a bride at last? I, who had been predicted never to marry?

As the singer began our wedding song, my mind flashed back through the events of life that brought me to this point. I never imagined that one childhood decision could set into motion a twenty-three-year conflict that would culminate in this wedding.

It all began one hot summer day when a pale green car packed with children slowed down on the bumpy country road in front of our home on the outskirts of the small town of Lodi, California. I stopped playing with my little sister and stared at the snowy-haired driver looking in our direction. Suddenly, he turned his car into our driveway and shut off the motor.

"Can we get out, too?" a freckled-faced boy called, hanging out of the window.

"No. I'll be just a minute; then I'll take you home," the man said as he emerged from the car and approached my sister and me.

"Aw! But I'm scrunched in here!" a voice protested from under the pile of kids stacked two and three deep in the backseat.

"Hello, little girl," the kind-faced gentleman said, squatting down to my level. "What's your name?"

"Patsy."

"And how old are you, Patsy?"

"Six."

"Is this your little sister?" He smiled at Delphine, who held her doll by one leg.

I nodded. "She's three. An' I have a big brother, too."

"Well, Patsy, is your father or mother home today?"

I looked up and saw my father, a short man in a safari hat, coming toward us pushing a wheelbarrow full of vegetables from the field.

"Here comes my daddy," I said, pointing.

The gentleman stood to meet my father. Daddy wiped his sweating hands on his pants before he shook the man's extended hand.

"Hello. My name is Reverend Smith."

"I'm Eddie Hirasuna."

"Are you new in this area?"

"Yeah. About four months."

"Welcome to the neighborhood! I have a Christian church about two miles from here. I wonder if you would allow your children to attend."

"We're Buddhists, you know," Daddy told the minister. "But our church hasn't begun a program for kids yet, since we came back to California from the relocation camp."

"Oh yes. Our country made a shameful error putting Japanese-American citizens into those camps during the war."

"Stop pinchin' me! I'm tellin' on you!" someone yelled from inside the car.

The minister moved toward the car, but continued to talk with Daddy. "Some of your Buddhist neighbors are letting their children attend my church." He pointed to the Japanese-American children in the car.

Daddy glanced at their faces, then turned to me. "You want to go, too?" he asked.

I nodded eagerly, not knowing what church was, but ready to go anywhere.

"OK, you can take my kids," Daddy said to the man.

Beginning the next Sunday, my older brother, Lester, and I went with Reverend Smith to his church. He conducted it in his one-car garage. Later, as the church grew, he moved it into a new chapel.

Reverend and Mrs. Smith's teenaged daughter, Joanne, was my Sunday school teacher. She taught us songs and told us stories about a man named Jesus.

At first I thought Jesus was only a storybook character, like the fairy-tale characters on my bedroom wallpaper. But after watching and listening to Joanne, I realized that he was an invisible friend to her. She knew him personally and talked with him every day.

What if Jesus is a real person? My mind swirled with intrigue.

As I attended Sunday school for the next two years, my heart slowly understood that not only was Jesus a real person, but he knew me and loved me, even when I was bad. In fact, he loved me so much he let people nail him to a cross to be punished for my sins. I couldn't keep back the tears as I listened to Joanne tell the class what Jesus had done for us.

By age eight, I had one all-consuming wish. I wanted to know Jesus as Joanne did. She often told us that we could know him for ourselves if we would invite him into our hearts as Savior and Lord.

I want to! I want to! I would cry inside, but shyness kept me from speaking out. Then one Sunday I felt a gentle tug deep inside of me. It was sweet and irresistible. *Could it be Jesus?* I thought, and tingled with wonder.

"Children, put your crayons away and get ready to go," Joanne said. "And if you want to have Jesus come into your heart today, please stay after class and I will pray with you."

The other children scrambled to the door, but I determined this time not to leave without Jesus. After the last classmate filed out of the room I timidly pulled at Joanne's sleeve.

"I want to have Jesus in my heart," I said, looking up into her eyes.

"Oh, Patsy!" she exclaimed, hugging me.

We sat at the table again. She opened her Bible to John 3:16 and explained it to me:

"God loved you so much, Patsy, that he sent his only begotten Son, Jesus, to die on the cross for your sins. If you believe in him, you will not perish but have everlasting life in heaven." Joanne turned to me. "Patsy, do you believe that Jesus died on the cross for your sins and that he wants to come into your heart to be your Savior?"

"Yes." I nodded.

We knelt together on the wooden floor. Joanne put her arm around my shoulders and had me repeat a simple prayer after her. Solemnly, I asked Jesus to forgive my sins and come into my heart as my Savior and Lord.

That day when Reverend Smith brought me home from church I jumped out of his car and ran as fast as I could into the house. The old screen door slammed behind me as I raced into the small kitchen.

"Mommy! Mommy! Guess what!" I exclaimed.

My mother had come in from the field to prepare lunch for the family. Her thick, black hair was matted down from wearing a hat under the hot sun. She stopped stirring vegetables in the frying pan and looked up. "What?" she responded, smiling at my excitement.

"Today I asked Jesus into my heart! See this Bible? Reverend Smith gave it to me, because now I belong to Jesus!" Beaming, I held up my new Bible for her to see.

My mother's smile disappeared. Alarm filled her eyes.

"What? You're too young to choose a religion for yourself!"

Stunned by her displeased reaction, I stammered,

"B-but . . ."

"You don't understand grown-up things yet. We are Japanese, and Japanese are Buddhists."

I felt confused.

"Daddy and I let you kids go to the Christian church to learn to be good children—not to become Christians!"

I couldn't understand why she was so upset. The adults at church were happy for me. Feeling crushed, unable to speak, I looked down at the floor.

My mother's voice softened. "I heard that the Buddhist church will begin a Sunday school for children soon. Then you can go there with all the other Japanese kids."

Going to church with all Japanese kids sounded like a nice idea to me. *I should be happy,* I told myself. Yet I wondered why my insides seemed to resist.

"Go change your clothes and set the table for lunch," my mother said as she turned her attention back to the stove. "And until you're old enough to tell the difference between what's real and what's imaginary, you'd better forget about choosing a religion."

Bewildered, I went to my room and slumped down on the bed. *Did I just imagine that Jesus was in my heart?* I wondered. *Am I too young to know the difference between what's real and what's not real?* I looked at the fairy-tale characters on the wallpaper. *I know they're not real. Is it possible that Jesus isn't real either?*

Then I remembered what Joanne had said: I could talk with Jesus, because he now lived in my heart. Hesitantly, I pulled open my collar and whispered into my blouse, "Jesus, are you in there?"

In a moment, I became aware of the presence of Someone else inside of me—Someone wonderful who loved me!

"Oh, Jesus!" I whispered in awe. I closed my eyes, cupped my hands over my heart, and sighed, "You're here, Jesus! You really are here with me!" Tears of relief trickled over my cheeks.

In the months that followed, I couldn't refrain from talking about Jesus. But my family and other relatives shook their heads in concern. "It's not normal for a child to be so religious," they said.

When the Buddhist Sunday school opened, my parents sent me there. Part of me felt comfortable among my Japanese peers, but at the same time I felt lonely inside. Jesus didn't seem to be there with me.

After many weeks, I guessed at what might be my problem. "I think Jesus was a Christian. And I think he wants me to go only to a Christian church," I told my mother.

"Nonsense! The same God stands behind all religions, and he doesn't mind which church you attend."

Somehow her answer seemed to choke me inside.

"All the other Japanese kids who went to the Christian church with you changed to the Buddhist church with no problem. I don't see why you can't, too," she continued.

I hung my head.

"Do you think you're smarter than Japanese grown-ups who go to the Buddhist church?"

"No, but I belong to Jesus, and I can't go back to the Buddhist church anymore," I said, my voice shaking.

"All right! I won't force you to go, but I don't want you to even mention Jesus in this house. Remember, this is a Buddhist home."

A worried look clouded her face. "And don't come crying to me when you grow up and no one marries you because you didn't go where other Japanese people go," she said as she left the room.

"Mommy!" I cried after her, feeling misunderstood and abandoned.

For weeks, I didn't attend any church. Then one Sunday, Reverend and Mrs. Smith and Joanne dropped in to say hello. Joanne had returned from college for the weekend and wanted to see me. They invited me back to church, and my parents allowed me to attend the Christian church again.

Soon after, however, the Smiths moved to another town and other ministers came. It was never
the same without the Smiths there to welcome me
with a warm hug. Then a few years later the chapel
closed altogether. Suddenly, I found myself isolated
in a home and ethnic environment allowing no
place for my Jesus.

The reality of Jesus in my heart clashed with my
Japanese-American heritage. In our little town, the
Japanese-American community revolved around the
Buddhist church. I was a child, caught in the mid-
dle, with no one to understand the conflict that tore
me apart inside.

In the churchless years that followed, I felt myself
losing touch with Jesus. Desperately, I tried to cling
to him, pleading, "Jesus, don't leave me!"

In my loneliness, I began to take my Bible to bed
with me. Clutching it to myself, I slept with it night
after night until the cover and pages frayed on the
edges.

But the day came when I couldn't feel his presence anymore, and I wondered if I had been delud-
ing myself all along. Feeling deserted and alone, I
wept into my pillow. "Oh, Jesus! Where are you?
Please don't leave me!"

Sorrowfully, I pulled my tattered Bible from its
hiding place under the mattress. At first, the volume

of printed pages without pictures overwhelmed me. Then I noticed a sentence that seemed to stand out on the page: "I will never leave thee, nor forsake thee."*

Somehow these words scooped me up and tenderly comforted me like a loving parent would a small child. I underlined the words with a pencil, and whenever I became afraid that Jesus had left me, I would run to that verse and let it hold me.

I began to keep a flashlight in my bed with my Bible. On nights when fears and doubts tormented me, I would crawl down under the blanket and find that underlined verse with my flashlight. It never failed to soothe and reassure me that I was God's own child.

In this way, I secretively began my lifelong relationship with the One I had chosen to be my first love.

*Hebrews 13:15b, KJV

TWO

Promises

In my high school days, kids who didn't fit in were called "squares." No one ever called me that to my face. Yet socially I always felt like a square peg trying to squeeze into a round hole.

Occasionally my Japanese-American friends would encourage me to attend Buddhist youth socials. "It's OK to come, even if you're a Christian," they would say. But when I went, I felt like a visitor—never one of them. And when I attended Christian youth activities I felt I looked out-of-place being the only Japanese-American in the crowd. Wherever I went I seemed to be different. But inside I was a typical teenage girl who desperately needed to feel like part of the group.

When my girlfriends and I got together, our discussions usually centered around our favorite subject—boys. We could talk for hours about the handsome guy on campus who we were certain had winked at us. Sometimes we would share our dreams for the future and talk about the kind of men we hoped to marry.

"He must be tall, handsome, romantic, rich, intelligent, thoughtful, kind, and lots of fun," we would agree. "Yeah!"

But while my mind danced at the thought of such a perfect Prince Charming, a vague discontent gnawed at my heart. Something was missing. But what more could any girl ask for in a husband?

One day I asked Louise, a Christian girlfriend, about her standards for a future husband. She thought for a moment, then answered, "First of all, the man I marry must know and love Jesus."

How interesting! I pondered on her unusual criteria and wondered why it should be so important. Slowly the answer dawned on me. *Something divine. Something eternal.* There it was! The missing element in my dream of a future husband—God himself!

Then I realized that not only was God missing from my dreams of a future husband, but lately he seemed to be missing in me, too. Somehow, during the years away from church, my delight in him had been replaced with an underlying boredom, a restlessness deep within me. My warm relationship with him had diminished to a cold set of burdensome rules.

My heart began to yearn once more for the sense of God's fulfilling presence. And that day, I determined to get closer to him. But no matter how hard I tried, without a church and without anyone to teach me how to know God better, I continued to slip further away from him.

I entered college, fearing I would lose him altogether before I graduated. I felt vulnerable, afraid the classes that taught godless philosophies would convince me that God didn't exist after all.

In late October, Louise invited me to a weekend Christian retreat for college students. I went, hoping it would help me get closer to God.

All weekend, the speakers explained vital truths about the Christian life. For the first time, I learned that God had a specific purpose and plan for my life. His plan was not based on a list of cold rules, but on a warm, growing relationship with him. I listened eagerly as the speaker expounded on ways I could develop that relationship. One vital point was to give God control over each area of my life.

To give God control of my life. How good that sounded to my weary soul, which had tried so hard to hang on to him!

That night, I hiked alone away from the campground. Sitting on a boulder overlooking a moonlit lake surrounded by mountains, I bowed my head and prayed.

"Jesus, more than anything else in the world, I want my relationship with you to grow. Please take control of my life." I sighed, wondering if he even heard my words. "Please, God! I can't bear to go on without you!" I cried. "I need you to guide me!" A cool breeze swished around me. I drew my knees up against my chest and buried my face in my arms.

After a long while, I thought I felt something bubbling up within me—like a tiny fountain in the depths of my being. Its springs rose higher and higher, until tears of joy poured over my face. Suddenly, the reality of Jesus' faithful love burst through the stagnation that had so long oppressed me. I felt like a butterfly set free from its confining cocoon. My heart soared with the sheer delight of rediscovering Jesus.

"Oh, Jesus! I love you!" I exclaimed, looking up into the starry sky. The scent of pine trees in the clear mountain air refreshed all my senses, and my world seemed incredibly alive. What an exciting future I faced!

"Lord Jesus, do you really have a plan for my life? I want you to know that I'll be whatever you want me to be! I'll go wherever you want me to go! And I'll marry whoever you want me to marry!"

Returning from the retreat, I joined a Christian group on campus. With their help I learned how to study the Bible, how to know God better, and how to discover what he wanted me to do with my life. Like a child just beginning to walk, I often fell and stumbled along on my wobbly spiritual legs. But slowly I began to develop a personal relationship with Jesus and to recognize God's guidance in my life. In the years that followed, God led me step by step into a teaching career.

During those same years, he was teaching me about the kind of man he wanted me to marry. In 2 Corinthians 6:14-18 he instructed me, as his child, to marry only another Christian, so we would have a divine basis for harmony in our life together. Through 1 Corinthians 2:14 he gently reminded me that the invisible world of God seems foolish to a person who hasn't personally met Jesus.

How well I knew this was so. All my Christian life I had tasted the loneliness of living in a "world that didn't exist" to those I loved the most. Shuddering at the thought of being married to a man who wouldn't be able to understand or share in my world with God, I carefully screened out each suitor not interested in knowing Jesus. And for each one who knew him, I asked God if he were my chosen husband.

The answer always seemed to be no.

When I was twenty-five years old, God led me to teach English in Japan. I spent the most fascinating three years of my life there, seeing and experiencing Japanese customs through my American mentality. One of these customs was matchmaking for marriage, which is still widely practiced in Japan.

One day Keiko, a college-age English Conversation student, came to practice speaking English with me. Bolder and more inquisitive than any of my other students, she always kept our sessions lively.

"What shall we talk about today?" I asked her after she settled herself in the chair across the narrow classroom table.

"I want to talk about malliage," she said, pronouncing her *r*'s like *l*'s.

"Marriage, *rr, rr,*" I corrected her.

"Mar-liage," she said contorting her mouth to articulate an *r*. "I want to know if you want mar-liage someday."

"Yes, I want to marry someday," I answered, thinking, *It's just like Keiko to ask such a forward question.*

"In Japan, it is custom to find a husband by . . . by . . . what you say . . . a mar-liage bloka."

Unable to understand, I looked at her blankly.

"You know . . . mar-liage bro-ka," she tried again.

"Oh! A marriage broker! In America we call that person a matchmaker."

"If you want mar-liage, I find a good matching maka' for you."

"That's very kind of you, Keiko," I said politely, "but Americans like to find their own mates and marry for love."

"Yes, you can mally for love! You tell matching maka' what kind of man you love. Then he find that man and bring him and his parents to you."

His parents, too! What a terrible pressure! I thought to myself. However, to Keiko I replied, "That would be convenient, but I already have a matchmaker. God is my matchmaker." I pointed toward heaven to help her comprehend what I was saying.

But two years later when I returned to America I was still single. My old friends had married and moved away, and I felt socially left behind. Furthermore, God led me back to my former teaching job near my parents' home, and I found myself living with them on the farm again.

Sometimes in the lull of classroom duties, my mind would recall an unforgettable experience I had in Japan just before I returned to America. In the middle of the night I had suddenly awakened, somehow knowing that the man God had planned for me to marry was in danger. He would die if I didn't pray for him. I prayed urgently until peace came.

What had happened to that man? Where could he be now? I wondered if I should change careers so I could go somewhere else to find him. But my heart knew better. God had picked this teaching position in the country for me. If I moved, I would only find myself in the wrong place at the wrong time.

During the Christmas holidays before my twenty-ninth birthday, I wistfully watched couples walk hand-in-hand through the shopping malls. I began to doubt that God had planned for me to marry at all.

When I came home from the shopping mall, I discovered a Christmas card waiting for me in the mail. "Oh, it's Keiko!" I exclaimed, immediately opening the card and reading her note inside:

Dear Patsy-Sensei,

  It has been six months since you returned to America. How have you been?

  Once when I inquired about your marrying, you said that God was your matchmaker, and he

*will find a husband for you someday. Please
don't think me rude for asking, but has your
God found you a husband yet? . . .*

"No, he hasn't," I said quietly to myself. I closed
the card. "No, he hasn't . . . not yet. . . ."

THREE

Matched for Marriage

"Poor Patsy! She thought her Christian God would find her a husband, but look where it got her. She'll probably never marry."

I overheard my relatives' casual comments at their annual gathering during the Christmas holidays. This remark pierced my heart. I could hardly wait to go home and cry out my pain to God.

When at last I sought refuge in my room, I threw myself on the bed and sobbed into the pillow. "Lord Jesus, they're talking about you and me! They're saying it's your fault that I'm not married!"

I wished I hadn't told anyone that I was waiting for God to bring me a husband. But I had presumed he would. Now I felt embarrassed that I had laid God's reputation on my presumptions.

"Lord, I don't mind remaining single, if that's

what you know is best for me. But please do something to vindicate your reputation!"

I began to think of ways I might be able to meet some men. But it was no use—all the Japanese-American men I had ever met were either Buddhists or unbelievers.

I ached inside at the seeming hopelessness of my situation, and wept into the pillow again. "Jesus, even if there were a Japanese-American Christian man somewhere, how will he find me, living way out here in the countryside . . . unless you somehow lead him to my door?"

Unexpectedly, in that instant my heart clearly understood that God had revealed his plan for me through my own mouth. "To my door? Jesus, you're going to bring a man for me to marry to my door?" I asked in amazement. Waves of peace flowed over me, and I knew beyond doubt that someday God would lead my future husband here to me.

That night, I was still chuckling inside when I shut off the light and climbed into bed. "Well, I guess I shouldn't be so surprised. My life has never been ordinary since you came along, Lord." Hugging my pillow, I fell peacefully asleep.

The next thing I knew, my bedroom door flew open, the light was switched on, and my mother was excitedly calling my name.

"Patsy, wake up!"

I sat up and glanced toward the window. *Still dark outside.* I reached for my glasses and squinted at the clock. *Six-thirty in the morning! No wonder it's dark!*

"What happened?" I mumbled.

"Chiyeko's on the phone and wants to know if she can bring a man here to meet you tonight."

My eyes opened wide. *A man? God said he would bring a man to my door. But so soon?*

"What do you want to do?" Mom asked. "Chiyeko is waiting. She has to call the man's mother with your answer."

"His mother? Why his mother?"

"That's the way she's supposed to introduce a couple for marriage."

"Huh?" I rubbed my eyes.

"Chiyeko is matching you for marriage in the formal Japanese way."

My mind swirled. *I must be dreaming! Nobody gets matched for marriage any more! Not in America! Not in the 1970s! How could this be happening to me?*

Then my thoughts flashed back to a day about five months before. While shopping at the local drugstore I had bumped into Chiyeko, a close friend of my mother's.

"Someday, I'd like to introduce you to a nice man

33

I know," she had said. But she hadn't said anything about putting me through an old-fashioned Japanese match for marriage.

"Well, hurry and decide," Mom urged. "Chiyeko has to make the arrangements before she goes to work this morning."

Lord, what shall I say? I asked silently, and again remembered the promise God had given me the night before. Chiyeko and her husband weren't Christians . . . but what if their friend was?

"Chiyeko is waiting!" Mom prodded me.

"Oh, . . . OK, tell her I'll meet him," I heard myself say.

Mom ran back to the phone in the kitchen.

Dazed, I sat on my bed and listened to the excited intonation of her voice as she worked out the details with Chiyeko.

After several minutes she hung up the phone and related the news to Dad. She quickly informed me that Chiyeko would bring the man and his widowed mother to our house at seven o'clock tonight. Moments later I heard her car speed away toward the plant nursery. Soon after, Dad's van chugged out of the yard toward his gardening clients in town.

Still sitting on my bed, I stared over at the teacher's manuals piled on my desk. The special assignments I had planned to prepare during Christmas vacation seemed unimportant now.

A restless wind pushed tree branches in scratchy patterns across the window above my desk and drew my attention outdoors. Lost in thought, I got up to look at the day. Low, threatening clouds blackened the sky. I shivered, and doubt slowly crept into my mind.

"Dear Jesus, what have I gotten myself into?" My voice came out in a dry whisper. "Maybe this man doesn't know you. What if he has no place in his life for you? Or he feels uncomfortable just hearing your name?"

A familiar feeling of isolation crept into my heart.

"Jesus, what made me think that people who don't know you would bring a man who does?" Regretting my presumptuous decision, I struggled into a sweatshirt and jeans.

The wind howled around the house, and tree branches screeched across the windowpane again. The wintry weather dampened my thoughts, and as the seriousness of the situation I had agreed to slowly dawned on me, regret swelled into frustration. Confused, I groaned, "Heavenly Father, please help me out of this mess!" But I heard no answer, only the gusty winds outside blowing against the trees.

Later, at breakfast, a thought flitted through my

mind: *God likes to do impossible things.*

I knew he could do anything. But somehow on this gloomy day, I couldn't believe that he had chosen tonight for the time to bring my future husband to my door. Maybe it wasn't impossible, but at least highly unlikely.

God likes to do impossible things! The same thought popped into my mind again, like a spark to kindle hope. But I quickly snuffed it out, afraid to hope in vain.

Then the thought returned a third time, and I finally recognized the voice of God in the idea that I had tried to dismiss. It burned itself into my heart. *Patsy, I enjoy doing impossible things for you. Give me a chance.*

Slowly, I began to wonder. Maybe this man really was my future husband! After all, he was being brought to my door.

Throughout the morning, that tiny flame of hope grew and gradually consumed my doubts and fears. Deep within, I felt assured that, however it turned out, at least God had arranged this special encounter.

That afternoon, while busily vacuuming the entryway of the living room, I happen to look at the door and a powerful intuition struck me: *In a few hours, my future husband will walk through that doorway!* I wondered what he would look like.

"Jesus, one thing's for sure. I'll know he's from you by the glow of your life shining through his eyes."

Joy bubbled within me, and I pranced with the vacuum cleaner through the rest of the house.

In the evening, my parents and I ate supper and quickly cleared the dishes. By six-thirty I was already dressed in my favorite white blouse and burgundy jumper and had nothing left to do but wait. Unable to sit still, I roamed into the family room and saw Dad sitting in his favorite chair, already changed into his best casual clothes, engrossed in the newspaper.

Suddenly my youngest sister, Diane, bounded into the house. Before I had a chance to ask why she had come home from her college apartment, she blurted out, "Are they still coming tonight?"

"Who told you?" I asked, somewhat chagrined with her visible enthusiasm over the coming meeting when I was trying so hard to remain calm.

"Mom did. I called a little while ago to find out what's going on at home. She said you were getting ready to meet someone to marry."

Diane looked over the refreshments on the kitchen counter, then stuck her head in the refrigerator. "Aren't you leery about being matched up with a total stranger?" she asked as she emerged with an apple.

"No," I said, trying to sound nonchalant.

"But what are you gonna do if he's weird?"

"I don't have to marry him if I don't like him."

Diane didn't seem to notice the quaver in my voice. She had situated herself by the kitchen window and was peering out at the country road in front of our home.

"Headlights!" she exclaimed suddenly.

I jumped up from the couch and ran to the window, only to see a truck flash by.

"Why don't you sit down, Diane? You're making me nervous!" I protested, but she continued to watch the road.

"Wait! This one's slowing down. I think it's them!"

I whirled around and saw headlights turn into our driveway.

"They're here!" Diane shouted loudly enough to be heard throughout the house.

My heart pounded, and my stomach fluttered like a thousand butterflies taking flight. If I had correctly interpreted what I thought God was telling me this morning, I was about to meet my future husband. That meant he *had* to love Jesus as I did. But as the next few seconds ticked away I struggled against a rising sense of anxiety. What if I was wrong? I took a deep breath to calm myself.

Dad folded his newspaper and pulled himself out

of his reclining chair. Mom hurried up the hall. Soon all of us waited in the living room, listening, tense with anticipation.

Car doors closed. Footsteps approached on the walkway. Shoes shuffled on the porch. The doorbell rang.

I hoped no one would notice my knees were shaking as I walked forward and self-consciously opened the door. There on the dimly lit porch stood Chiyeko and her husband, Tom, and behind them, my prospective husband and his mother.

"Please come in," I said.

Smiling cordially, they stepped into our living room. I tried not to stare at the man who had been brought for me. But several stolen glances revealed a pleasant-looking man of medium height and build with black-rimmed glasses and abundant, neatly combed black hair. I approved.

"Patsy, this is Walter Oda," Chiyeko said. "Walter, this is Patsy Hirasuna."

"I'm pleased to meet you," he said, appearing a bit nervous, but extending his hand to me.

"I'm pleased to meet you, too," I responded, placing my hand in his, surprised at my own calmness.

I looked into his eyes, almost expecting to sense a kindred spirit of one who knew and loved my God, too. But I was startled to detect an emptiness deep within him. An inner chill shook me, smothering the tiny flame of hope that had grown stronger throughout the day—that this was the man God had promised me.

Chiyeko introduced everyone else. A round of handshaking mixed with Japanese bowing followed, and Mom seated the guests in the living room. Diane hung their coats while I slipped out of the room to bring refreshments.

Alone in the kitchen I stared, trembling, through the window at the cold, black night. Finally, my voice choked out what my heart feared. "Jesus, he doesn't know you, does he?" I whispered brokenly, fighting back tears of disillusionment. Just because God had given me a special promise, I had assumed that this meeting would fulfill my hopes for the future. Now, once again, I felt ashamed of my presumption. The last thing I wanted to do was go back and face those people in the next room. *Jesus, please help me.* I sent up a silent prayer of desperation.

After I regained my composure I picked up the tray and returned to the living room, where the older folks chatted in Japanese like longtime friends. Diane sat on the carpet across the coffee table from Walter.

"You live in Tacoma, Washington?" I overheard Diane exclaim. "What brings you to California?"

"I'm just here for the holidays, visiting my mother in Sacramento," Walter answered.

I set a bowl of rice crackers on the coffee table and began to serve hot green tea and cake. I could feel Walter glancing at me as I served the others. Finally, I set tea and cake on the coffee table before him and seated myself on the couch.

"Patsy, I understand you're an elementary schoolteacher," he said in a quiet, pleasant voice.

"Yes, I teach third grade. What kind of work do you do, Walter?" I asked, wondering what he thought of me.

"I'm an electrical engineer."

"That's a nice profession," I said and suddenly realized I didn't know what else to say. Feeling uneasy, I began to sip at my tea. He leaned forward and began to eat his cake, using the fork with his left hand. We ate without a word, smiling at each other when our eyes met accidently.

After he finished the cake, he looked at me and said, "Diane tells me you taught in Japan for three years."

"Yes. I just came back six months ago," I answered, relieved that the silence was broken.

"Did you take many pictures there?"

"Yes. Would you like to see some of them?"

"Yes, I would."

I brought my album and sat next to him. Our conversation became less strained as he turned the

pages and I explained the highlights of my life in
Japan—teaching English and working with
missionaries.

I yearned to have him tell me that he had come
because God had sent him to me. But even when I
disclosed that I had gone to Japan because I felt
God wanted me to go, he said nothing. The blank
response in his eyes convinced me that he didn't
know God at all. By the time my album ended, so
did my hope that God had sent Walter to me.

For the rest of the evening I tried hard to hide my
disappointment. Fortunately Diane, my ever-talk-
ative sister, kept the conversation going.

At last, the guests stood up to leave. But before
he left, Walter asked me to have dinner with him
two evenings later. His mother gave me a gracious,
approving smile as they all walked out the door.

No sooner did I close the door than Diane asked,
"Well, what do you think of him?"

"He seems nice," I managed to say before a lump
closed in on my throat.

"I think he's suitable for Patsy," Mom
commented.

"Is he that strange?" Diane joked. I forced a smile
at my sister's friendly teasing.

"I mean they're suitable in age, height, education,
and family background," Mom continued.

"Dad, what do you think of Walter?" I asked,

hoping that my father had noticed something negative about his prospective son-in-law.

"He's a good man," Dad stated, and then he walked back to the family room to finish his newspaper.

"If you get engaged now you could be a June bride as soon as school's out," Diane coaxed.

"Diane, don't push her!" Mom scolded. "Now it's up to them to get to know each other and decide if they want to get married."

Mom turned to me. "Think it over carefully. If you decide you don't want to marry him, you'd better tell him as soon as possible. I understand he's thirty-three years old. You should both look for someone else if you're not interested in each other."

"OK, Mom," I said and started to gather the teacups and dishes and carry them to the kitchen. Mom and Diane picked up the remainder of the refreshments and followed me.

The discussion continued in the kitchen, but in my heart I had already decided that Walter was not the man for me. I knew I couldn't marry him. And I knew I would have to tell him so on our dinner date.

FOUR

Farewell Date

"Lord, Walter will be here in two minutes, and I still have no idea how I'm going to tell him I've already decided not to marry him. What'll I do?"

Just tell him the truth—that your God forbids you to marry a non-Christian, God seemed to say to my heart.

"But, Lord, he won't understand that. He'll think I'm a religious fanatic," I protested. "Can't you have him reject me first, so I don't have to tell him?"

The doorbell rang.

I made one more plea. "Lord, please don't let him be interested in me!"

When I opened the door, Walter's clothes immediately caught my attention. Everything he wore appeared brand new—his navy blue sport coat, paisley tie, checked slacks, and even his shiny, black shoes.

I gulped.

"Hi, Patsy," he said with a beaming smile.

"Hi," I said weakly, feeling circumstances closing in on me.

We drove for an hour to a Sacramento restaurant where waiters in black tuxedos attended to our every wish. The food, atmosphere, and service were exquisite. But I couldn't enjoy a bit of it. My mind tormented me with the puzzling obsession: *How can I break the news to Walter? Especially when he seems to be interested in me already!*

Several times, I opened my mouth to tell him. But somehow every time words came out, I heard myself comment on the "lovely restaurant."

"Is everything all right with you tonight?" Walter asked with concern in his voice.

"Oh, I'm fine, thank you," I said, touched by his sensitivity, which caused me to feel even worse.

As we stood up to leave, Walter said, "I hope you enjoyed your dinner."

"It was delicious," I said. But when I saw the mess on my plate I wanted to hide myself under the table. It looked as if I had stirred my food all evening and hadn't eaten any of it.

Thick fog had rolled into the city while we were in the restaurant. Walter drove slowly, peering intently through the whiteness. Aside from an occasional comment about the fog, we rode in what seemed an eternity of silence.

My chances to tell him are slipping away! I fretted. *I can't let him go back to Tacoma with false hopes of seeing me again!*

A few miles from home, I felt I would explode if I didn't tell him what I had to say.

"Walter, there's something important I have to tell you," I blurted out.

"OK, but could it wait until we get to your home? I want to concentrate on the road right now."

"Oh, . . . sure." I sat back in the seat, embarrassed. *How could I be so thoughtless?* I mentally berated myself.

Finally, we arrived home. He shut off the motor and turned to me. "Now, you can tell me what you wanted to say." The serious tone in his voice told me that he partly expected bad news.

"Would you mind if we talked in the house for a few minutes?" I asked, suddenly unprepared to speak.

"OK."

My parents and sister had gone to bed. I invited Walter into the family room where we could talk without waking anyone. We sat on the couch. Walter waited patiently as I struggled to find the gentlest way to tell him.

At last I said, "I guess you know I'm a Christian by the pictures of my church activities in Japan. But did you know that Christians are to marry only other Christians?"

"No, I didn't," he said quietly, as if he understood already where this conversation would end.

I looked down at my hands, sticky with perspiration. *Now what do I say, Lord?*

"Well, I guess, first, I need to know if you're a Christian," I said hesitantly.

"No, I'm not," he answered in his characteristic brief manner.

"I was afraid you weren't," I said, unable to look up. "That means I can't marry you. . . . Not that you would have even asked me to," I stammered, embarrassed again.

Walter made no comment. *What does he think of me now? Why doesn't he say something?*

"I don't want to lead you on or keep you from meeting someone else to marry. What I mean is, I think it's best for us to go our separate ways before we get to know each other any better," I concluded.

Frowning, he fixed his eyes on the dying embers in the fireplace across the room. After a long while, he spoke.

"Why did you decide to meet me when you weren't sure I was a Christian?"

I hung my head. "I'm sorry, but I mistook you for the husband that God said he would bring to my door."

"God talked to you?" Walter sounded surprised.

"No, not the way you think."

"What do you mean, then?"

"It's a long story. Are you sure you want to hear it?"

"Yes, I do."

Reluctantly, I told him what had happened on the night before I met him. He listened, enraptured, like a child engrossed in a bedtime tale.

When I finished, Walter shook his head in wonder. "That's amazing!" he said. "But I still want to know how God spoke to you. Did you hear a voice?"

"No, it wasn't an audible voice. It was more like a silent understanding between two hearts that have known and loved each other for a long time."

Walter stared at the floor and said nothing, and again a mixture of embarrassment and shame filled me.

49

"I'm really sorry that I put everyone through so much trouble," I said softly.

Stillness permeated the house. I waited for his reaction.

At last he stood up. "Thank you for your explanation," he said. He held out his hand to me. "I'm glad that I knew you even for a short time."

"So am I," I said, shaking his hand.

I walked him to the door. He opened it, said good-bye, and walked away. As the foggy darkness swallowed his frame from my sight I closed the door and leaned against it, staring blankly at the floor. Sadness swept over me. *Poor Walter! Such a nice man, living his whole life without God!*

The next morning, Diane intercepted me the minute I walked out of my bedroom. "Well, how was the date?"

"Fine."

"You gonna see him again before he goes back to Tacoma?"

"No, we don't have enough in common," I said, trying hard to sound casual.

"Mom, did you hear that? Patsy and Walter broke up already." Diane's news service reached the kitchen before I could stop her.

"What's the problem?" Mom asked when I entered the kitchen.

"Oh, he's not my type, and I'm not his type," I

said, not wanting to mention God and receive a lecture on being too religious.

"I hope you're not being too picky. You'll never find a perfect man."

"I know, Mom. But you said I should tell him as soon as possible if I thought he wasn't right for me. So I did."

After breakfast, I drove to the school. I needed something to do, a constructive project to keep myself busy. In my classroom, I faced the bare bulletin boards that had been stripped before Christmas vacation. I rolled up my sleeves and plunged into preparing new displays and lessons. For the next two days, I forced the challenges of my work to occupy all my thoughts and energy.

Sunday, the last day of Christmas vacation, appeared damp and dark. Diane and I were washing the lunch dishes when we saw Walter drive into the yard.

I gasped in disbelief.

"I thought you and Walter broke up!" Diane remarked, surprised. She glanced at me mischievously.

"I thought so, too," I said, hastily drying my hands on a dish towel. My head spun with questions. *God, why is he coming back? What am I to do now?*

Through the window, I watched him get out of

his car. A somber look clouded his face as he walked toward the house. Leaving Diane to finish the dishes, I went to answer the doorbell and soon stood face-to-face with the man I had thought I would never see again.

"Hello, Patsy. May I talk with you for a few minutes? I can't stay long. I have to return the car to my brother in San Jose before I catch a plane back to Tacoma."

"Please come in," I offered, hoping he wouldn't notice how nervous I was. I motioned for him to sit on the living room couch, and then closed the sliding door to the kitchen for extra privacy.

We sat in awkward silence for a moment. Then he began, "I've done a lot of thinking in the last four days. Somehow I feel that we must have met for more reasons than to say good-bye so soon. . . . If you don't mind, I'd like to keep in touch with you. Could we exchange letters?" Walter's eyes searched my face as he waited for an answer.

I stared at my hands and stalled for time as an unexpected confusion clouded my resolve not to get involved. I realized that part of me wanted very much to stay in touch with this man. Almost desperately I turned to the Lord for guidance. *Lord Jesus, what shall I say?*

"I don't mind corresponding with you, but I

don't want to get involved with anyone I can't marry," I finally replied.

"That shouldn't be a problem if we both understand we're writing just as friends."

His point sounded rational, and silently I chided myself for panicking over the simple act of writing letters.

"I suppose you're right," I conceded. "We could write to each other as friends and nothing more until one of us meets someone else. OK."

We smiled at each other as we came to an agreement. Then Walter looked at his watch and stood up.

"I've got to go now or I'll miss my plane. Please say 'hello' to your parents and Diane for me."

He hurried out to his car, calling back, "I'll write to you soon!"

Somewhat dazed, I waved good-bye and closed the door. *Jesus, what was that all about?* I questioned.

Before I had time to sort through this turn of events, the sliding door flew open and Diane rushed in. "Why'd he leave so fast?" she asked, almost breathless with excitement.

I drew a deep breath and tried to answer in a steady voice. "He had to catch a plane back to Tacoma."

Diane's eyes gleamed with the impatience of intense curiosity that only a younger sister can feel. "Well, what'd he come for?"

"Oh, he just wanted to know if I would write to him."

"You gonna?"

"I guess so."

Diane flashed me a deliberate grin. Her eyes gleamed. I sensed that I didn't look as nonchalant as I tried to sound.

"No, it's not what you think," I said reproachfully. "We're just writing as friends, until one of us meets someone to be serious about. Nothing more!"

"I thought you said you didn't have anything in common!" she teased.

"We don't. But that doesn't mean we can't exchange a few letters," I said in defense, although in my heart I still wondered why God would want us to correspond.

I put on my coat and walked outside behind the tractor shed to gaze westward over Dad's walnut orchard. Often, when I needed to talk with God, I would meet him in this place. Today our special spot was muddy—bare trees set against a dark sky.

"Lord, I don't understand what's going on!" I cried. "Why did you let him come back? What could we write about, anyway?" A huge raindrop plopped on my nose, but I determined to wait there for an answer from God.

No dramatic answer came—nothing but a velvety peace that erased all my noisy questions. I walked back to the house with the quiet assurance that, as in the past, I could trust God to guide me through this challenging situation.

FIVE

Just Pen Pals

January 4

Dear Patsy,

I'm happy that I met you during the holidays. You have a nice family and a beautiful home.

I made it to the airport in plenty of time to catch my plane.

Before I got this job in Tacoma four months ago, I worked in Sacramento for ten years and lived with my mother. Living alone in an apartment and cooking for myself are new experiences for me.

I'm glad you agreed to correspond with me. It'll be nice to come home to my quiet apartment and find a letter from you. Please write and tell me about yourself.

Sincerely,
Walter

January 12

Dear Walter,

Thank you for your letter. I, too, am glad that we met.

I'm impressed that you cook for yourself. Do you mind telling me what a bachelor prepares for dinner?

I don't know what to tell you about myself. I suppose I could start at the beginning. I was born in Arkansas in a relocation camp during the war.

After the war, my parents moved to Lodi and later purchased this farm. I grew up right here on this place. Several years ago, our present home was built on the same property where our old house used to be.

I had the typical childhood of a third-generation Japanese-American girl, except for one thing. When I was eight years old, I met God through Jesus Christ. And he has made my life a unique adventure with him.

I have one older brother, Lester, who owns a glass company in Fresno. His wife's name is Helen. I have two younger sisters—Delphine, a magazine editor in San Francisco, and Diane, a senior at Sacramento State.

Seven years ago, I graduated from Sacramento State with a teacher's certificate. I've been teaching ever since.

Now that you know "everything" about me, please write and tell me about yourself.

Always,
Patsy

January 20

Dear Patsy,

It was wonderful to hear from you.

I wish I could impress you by saying I'm a gourmet cook. But I must admit that my cooking skills are limited to rice, ramen, fried eggs, and meat loaf. Usually, I bake a meat loaf large enough to eat for several days, lunch and supper. Fortunately, I have friends who often invite me over for good, home-cooked dinners.

As for my life, I was born and raised on a farm in Sacramento. I have one sister (the oldest) and five brothers. I'm the second from the bottom and the only one not married. My father died while I was in college.

After graduating from the University of California at Berkeley twelve years ago, I worked as an electrical engineer in Sacramento, and now in Tacoma. When I'm not working, I enjoy fishing.

Thank you for telling me about your life. I was especially interested to read that you met God when you were only eight years old. Do you mind telling me how that happened?

I look forward to hearing from you again.

Sincerely,
Walter

January 26

Dear Walter,

I enjoyed reading about your life.

You may not be a gourmet cook, but if practice makes perfect you must make the tastiest meat loaves in Tacoma.

Would you believe that I met God in a one-car garage? When I was six years old, my parents allowed me to attend a Christian church conducted by Reverend A. A. Smith in his garage.

After attending for two years I realized that Jesus was the Son of God, who came to earth to die for my sins. And I discovered that I could know him personally, because he rose from the dead and is still alive today.

One Sunday, with the help of my Sunday school

*teacher, I prayed and invited Jesus into my heart.
Later at home, I sensed his presence within me and
began to talk with him.*

*From that day on, I somehow knew that God
had become my heavenly Father and heaven had
become my real homeland.*

*Enough said about me! Please tell me more
about yourself. How is electrical engineering? Are
you busy on a special project?*

Wishing you a nice day.

Always,
Patsy

February 5

Dear Patsy,

*I'm not "electrical engineering" today, because
the company is closed due to heavy snow.*

*I'm sitting in my apartment by the window,
watching the snow fall and rereading your letter. I
can't help but be fascinated by your special associ-
ation with God. Do many Christians talk with God
as you do?*

*I hope you don't mind my cutting this letter
short, but I want the postman to pick it up today.
The sooner I send it, the sooner you'll get it. And*

the sooner you get it, the sooner you'll answer. And the sooner you answer, the sooner I'll hear from you again.

Looking forward to your next letter.

Sincerely,
Walter

February 8

Dear Walter,

Are you still snowed in? I hope that didn't cause you many problems.

I will try to answer the question you asked in your last letter.

Every Christian has a reborn spirit that can communicate with God, his spiritual Father. But every Christian doesn't take the time to develop an intimate relationship with him.

God talks to us constantly. However, most of the time we don't quiet our hearts long enough to hear what he's saying.

It requires practice to learn to hear God accurately. I'm just beginning to learn. I still often "mishear" him—like the time I thought he told me that he was bringing you to my door to marry me.

May I ask what your experience with God has

been? I'm not snowed in, but I would enjoy hearing from you soon.

Have a nice snow vacation!

Always,
Patsy

February 16

Dear Patsy,

My snow vacation lasted three days. Your letter came on my third day back at work. Thank you for your quick response.

I've never had a personal encounter with God as you've experienced, but I believe that a superior being must have created this world.

As an electrical design engineer, it's hard for me to swallow the theory of evolution. All the incredible balance and deliberate design in nature couldn't have happened by accident. And I just can't believe that "chance" taught the animals what they know and do by instinct.

It's snowing again. Snowflakes remind me of something I once read. Every snowflake has its own unique design—no two are alike. That, too, tells me that there's a creative genius somewhere.

Just in case the company closes down again be-cause of snow, would you write again soon?

Sincerely,
Walter

February 24

Dear Walter,

Thank you for sharing your thoughts on God.

I was especially interested that you believe the miracles of nature are evidences of the existence of a Divine Creator. Did you know that God says he displays his handiworks in nature to confirm his ex-istence to the hearts of mankind?

God placed instincts in animals to guide them to obtain their greatest needs. Do you suppose he also placed an instinctive longing for God in our hearts, knowing he himself is our greatest need?

Pascal, the famous physicist and philosopher, said: "There is a God-shaped vacuum in the heart of each man which cannot be satisfied by any cre-ated thing but only by God, the Creator, made known through Jesus Christ."

I think he must be right. When I talk with people who have recently met Jesus Christ they tell me that the gnawing, empty hole inside their hearts disap-peared when he came in.

Looking forward to hearing from you again.

Always,
Patsy

March 12

Dear Patsy,

Before I began to correspond with you, it never occurred to me that ordinary people could know God personally. Perhaps someday, I may become interested enough to search the religions of the world to find him, too.

But until then, I'll just enjoy what you have to say on the subject. I care about what's important to you.

When I asked you to write me, I didn't expect to be as fascinated as I have been with your letters. Lately, I've been wondering if it's permissible for pen pals to sometimes visit each other in person.

I'm planning a trip to Sacramento to see my mother in two weeks. I'd like to see you, too. May I drop in to visit you?

Hoping you'll say yes.

Sincerely,
Walter

March 19

Dear Walter,

I'm glad you may consider searching for God someday. However, you don't have to search the whole world for him. He can be found as close as your own breath.

Until I took a college class on the religions of the world, I assumed all religions sought God. To my surprise, I discovered that many founders of great religions didn't even believe in the existence of God.

They searched for truths that would help mankind. They searched for answers about life after death. But many of them never searched for nor ever knew the living God.

God isn't a religious philosophy, nor a sacred feeling, nor a vague concept for our minds. He is an all-present, all-knowing, all-powerful Person, who loves us and wants to befriend us personally. And anyone who chooses to know him can do so.

Regarding your visit, I believe God gave me his approval to see you. One of the ways he guides his children through this life is with his peace. When I inquired about your coming, he filled my heart with his divine peace.

I'll be looking forward to seeing you soon.

Always,
Patsy

March 25

Dear Patsy,

You can't imagine how happy I was to know that even God approves of our getting together!

I'll fly into Sacramento this Friday night, and visit you on Saturday afternoon.

Looking forward to seeing you SOON!

Sincerely,
Walter

SIX

The Visit

The aroma of hot sukiyaki filled the kitchen. And was I hungry! I sat down at the table and glanced at the clock. *One thirty! I hope Walter doesn't come just as we start to eat,* I thought, as I scooped a spoonful of sukiyaki out of the cooking skillet in the middle of the table and eagerly bit into a tender, juicy piece of beef, flavored to perfection. Then I heard gravel crunch in the driveway.

Diane put down her chopsticks and peeked through the curtains. "Walter's here," she said to me across the table.

"Who's he?" our aunt asked.

"He's Patsy's boyfriend from Tacoma, Washington."

"He's not my boyfriend. He's just a guy I met over the Christmas holidays," I corrected.

"He must be interested in you if he comes to visit all the way from Washington," our uncle commented.

"No, he came back to see his mother who lives in Sacramento," I said, on my way to the front door.

"Bring him into the kitchen, so we can all meet him," my sister Delphine called from the table. "I haven't seen him yet either."

When I opened the door, Walter smiled and handed me a box of chocolates. "This is for you."

Oh, no! Now everyone will think he really is my boyfriend! I fretted, almost forgetting to thank him and to invite him in. He stepped into the living room, looking back at the cars in the yard. "I didn't know your family was having company today."

"It's just my uncle and aunt from Los Angeles visiting for the week. And my sisters are home for the weekend."

"Oh, you're still eating. I must be early," he said, checking his watch as I guided him to the kitchen.

"No, we're the ones off schedule," I said, and proceeded to introduce him to Uncle Tak, Auntie Yo, and Delphine.

"Walter, there's plenty of sukiyaki," Mom said.

"Sit down and eat," Dad invited.

"No, thank you. I ate just before I came. I'll go read some magazines." He stepped to the family-room end of the kitchen.

When I returned to my chair next to Auntie Yo, she jabbed my side with her elbow and whispered loudly, "Grab him, honey! He'll make you a good hubby!"

Delphine and Diane almost choked on their attempt to conceal laughter. I managed a weak smile and wondered if Walter had heard the comment. In dismay at the way his visit had started, I gulped down a few more bites of sukiyaki and excused myself from the table.

"Would you like to take a walk around the yard?" I asked Walter.

"OK," he said, smiling, and followed me out the front door.

Outside, spring peeped through every corner of the garden. The air felt clear and fresh. We strolled around to the backyard, stopping along the way to admire daffodils nodding their sunny faces at us. Walter paused in front of Mom's Japanese garden under a huge, leaning pine tree.

"I wish I had my camera so I could take a picture of you here," he said.

In spite of my deliberate detachment I felt a warm glow at his compliment. It had been a long time since a man had asked to take a picture of me. But I passed off the remark with a smile and led the way out toward the field.

"After Dad stopped vegetable farming, he planted

these cherry trees and some walnut trees in the back," I explained, pointing out the boundaries of my father's small farmland.

"I see." Walter's eyes scanned the country view appreciatively.

We walked together toward the walnut orchard on the other side of the tractor shed. The afternoon sun warmed our faces as we stood looking westward at the horizon beyond the walnut trees, dressed in young green leaves . . . beyond the wire fence of the neighbor's alfalfa field.

"I love this peaceful spot," I said, almost speaking to myself. "This is where I often come alone to talk with God." I glanced at him. He was watching me somberly, as usual, but with a friendly, interested light in his eyes. I hesitated, then said, "Actually, you're the only person I've ever told about this place."

I stopped abruptly, realizing I had allowed Walter into my private world with God. He smiled at me, and seemed pleased that I had shared with him my secret place. But I felt vulnerable and uneasy.

"Here, would you like to sit down?" I offered him an old crate that stood by the shed. I took another crate for myself. For a long while we just sat and watched robins fly among the trees.

"Do you always ask God about everything you do?" Walter's quiet voice broke the silence.

"I try to." I answered without looking at him.

"May I ask why?"

"Because he's God, and he knows what's best for me," I said, turning to watch his eyes as I spoke.

Walter gazed at me. "Patsy, you live in a fascinating world!"

I knew he meant that my world was unreal to him, and a familiar pain of isolation pricked my heart.

"I guess we Christians approach life differently—always asking God about everything," I said. "What do you do when you have to make an important decision?"

"What kind of decision?"

"Well, for instance, how would you decide who is the right woman for you to marry?" I held my breath, surprised by my sudden boldness.

Walter answered calmly. "That's easy. I would first analyze and calculate all the options. Then I would narrow it down to one best choice that my mind and heart agreed upon. Then I would propose to her." He stopped talking and winked at me.

I gulped. *Surely, he wasn't thinking of proposing to me!* Nervously, I rose and carried my crate back against the shed. Then I heard myself asking, "Have you analyzed many ladies yet? I mean, have you been meeting some interesting girls lately?"

"No. Friends try to match me up with girls, but I

always refuse. I want to see and know the girl first."
He picked up his crate and placed it next to mine.
His nearness disturbed me. I was finding it difficult
to remain detached.

"But you didn't see or know me beforehand.
Why'd you agree to meet me?" I stepped away from
him and looked across the field.

He came and stood beside me. "I really don't
know why. Chiyeko phoned awfully early that
morning. Maybe I was too sleepy to think up a
good reason not to meet you. Besides, I didn't have
anything else planned for the evening," he teased.

I gave him a half smile, determined not to encourage his advances.

But he put his hands on my arms and looked into
my eyes. "No matter why I agreed, I'm glad I came,
and I'm glad I met you, Patsy," he said.

He drew me to himself and held me in his arms.

Soft breezes blew through the pines, sounding
like distant streams. I felt warm and comfortable in
his arms, but my heart screamed in protest: *Back
away! Don't let yourself get involved! You'll slip
into his world without God!*

I knew I shouldn't let him hold me, but my arms
seemed too weak to push him away. *Oh, God!
Please help me!* I prayed.

"Patsy! Walter! Where are you?" Diane's voice

called from the other side of the shed.

"We're out here!" I called back, relieved, moving away from Walter.

Diane came around the side of the shed. "Mom wants to know if you care for some apple pie."

"I don't know about you, Walter, but I'm hungry for dessert," I said. My stomach reminded me that I had eaten hardly any lunch.

"It sounds good to me, too. Apple pie's my favorite."

We walked back to the house with Diane.

Later, while we ate pie in the living room, Auntie Yo came in from the kitchen. "I'm fixing my special roast duck and chow mein for tonight, honey," she said to me. "Why don't you ask Walter to stay for dinner?"

"Oh, I shouldn't . . . ," Walter began, looking at me.

"You're welcome to stay if you like," I said.

"Sure, honey, why don't you stay and eat with us?" Auntie Yo encouraged.

"Well, if it's really OK with you," Walter said, looking at me again.

"He'll stay." Diane decided for him.

Walter stayed for dinner and spent the evening watching TV with the family.

The others had gone to bed by the time I walked

him to the door to say good night.

"I don't know when I've had a nicer day, Patsy," he said, looking fondly at me.

"I enjoyed the day, too," I said, feeling guilty that I had liked his attention so much.

For a moment we stood looking at each other. But again I sensed the emptiness of his life without God. My heart ached. This relationship was futile. There could be no future for us. I turned my eyes away.

"I hope you'll let me visit you again," he said quietly.

"I . . . I'll keep writing to you," I stammered uncertainly, unable to tell him that I wouldn't see him again.

He placed his hand under my chin and lifted my face to his. Tenderly, he kissed my lips.

My heart flashed a warning: *Don't even begin to get involved!*

I tried to speak, but my mind threatened: *If you let him go, you'll never meet anyone else! Never!*

"Good night," he whispered. "I'll come back to see you soon."

Speechless, I watched him leave.

In my bedroom, I felt alone and distant from God. His peace had left me. I knew I shouldn't have let Walter go home with the impression that we might have a future together.

"Lord Jesus, I'm sorry for not speaking up," I said. But the afterglow of the lovely time with Walter tugged at my emotions. Sorrow filled me because I had lost God's peace, but I wasn't really sorry that I hadn't let go of Walter. *I can't let go of him and risk spending the rest of my life alone!* I thought. *He's probably my very last chance!* I flung myself on the bed and wept in misery.

Then, from the depths of my heart, God confronted me. "Patsy, can't you trust me any more with your future?"

In a flash, I understood my real offense toward God. True, I failed by not telling Walter to never return. But that was only the surface issue. My error went far deeper than that. I feared that God would withhold a good husband from me and leave me with no one.

This time my tears fell not for myself but for the God I had offended. "Lord, I'm sorry I hurt you. How could I distrust you when you've always treated me with such loving-kindness? You've never withheld any good thing from me. Please forgive me."

I looked up and fervently renewed my vows to him. "Lord Jesus, I love you! And I will trust you with my future, my marriage, and my life."

Gently, the sense of his presence returned, and his peace flooded my heart.

SEVEN

No Mere Book

April 3

Dear Patsy,

Thank you again for the wonderful time I enjoyed with you, your family, your uncle and aunt. Please extend my best regards to them all.

Especially thank your Aunt Yo for preparing the delicious dinner. By the way, I liked what I overheard her say to you at the lunch table.

After I came back to Tacoma, I caught a miserable cold. I don't think I care to tackle another winter here.

I thought of you all the way home on the plane. You are a very special person to me. I miss you and look forward to the time when I can see you again. Please write soon.

Sincerely,
Walter

April 10

Dear Walter,

How is your cold? I'm praying that you'll soon be fine.

When we decided to correspond, we agreed it would be on a friendship basis only. But your last visit and letter indicate a more serious relationship.

Walter, please understand that it's important to my life with God that I don't get involved with you. Let me try to explain.

As a Christian I have met God through his Son, Jesus Christ, who came to earth to relate to us in human flesh. Like any other relationship, a meaningful relationship with God must be developed by spending time together to listen, talk, and do things that please each other.

We please God when we trust him and obey what he says in his Book, the Bible. Concerning marriage, the Bible forbids a Christian to marry a non-Christian because they would be incompatible.

If I were to become involved with you, knowing it could lead to marriage, this would constitute willful disobedience to God. Disobedience always ruins our relationship with God. That is too great a price for me to pay in exchange for any human relationship.

I'd like to continue writing to you as a friend.

But if it's going to encourage you to think about marriage to me, I must insist we discontinue our correspondence immediately. I'll leave the decision to you.

Always,
Patsy

April 18

Dear Patsy,

As I analyzed what you wrote, I came to the unbelievable conclusion that we are being separated by a mere book. A book thousands of years old, no less.

I'll continue to write you as a friend because I'm curious to know how you could let an ancient book rule your life in this modern age. Times have changed. How can anything written that long ago give relevant advice to a person today? I don't understand.

My cold is much better. Thank you for your concern.

Please write again.

Sincerely,
your friend,
Walter

April 26

Dear Walter,

The book that has come between us is no mere book. The Bible is the only book in the world that God claims to have written.

In fact, God says this Book is himself in written form—revealing his accomplishments, his thoughts, his feelings, his will, his plans, and his personality.

Yes, times have changed. Fashions have changed. Human philosophies constantly change. But mankind is basically the same from the beginning. That's why God's "handbook for humans" is still as relevant today as it was thousands of years ago.

In this unstable world of ever-changing human ideologies and decaying morality, I have chosen the Creator God and his unchangeable Instruction Book as my absolute standard of conduct.

Walter, I'm glad you decided to continue writing to me as a friend. I would have missed your interesting letters if you had stopped.

Please write again soon.

Always,
Patsy

May 5

Dear Patsy,

Are you sure we're talking about the same book? While in college, I once tried to read the Bible.

Please don't be offended, but I couldn't get much out of it. In fact, I found it rather boring.

May I ask what makes you think the Bible was written by God? What proof do you have?

Before I close this letter, I have a favor to ask of you. Will you send me a picture of yourself?

Please answer soon.

> *Sincerely,*
> *Walter*

May 14

Dear Walter,

I'm sorry that you had a negative experience reading the Bible. But God wrote the Bible to the hearts of those who already know him. It reads like a letter to a stranger unless God lives in your heart, making it personal to you.

However, if you want to try reading the Bible again, read the Gospel of John in the New Testament. It speaks to those who don't know God, but want to be introduced to him.

Actually, no one else but God could have written the Bible. Who but God could have known the ingredients he used to make human bodies? Until recent years, even scientists didn't know that our bodies consist of the same chemical elements as the dust of the earth. The Bible said it long ago.

Who but God could have written the reason he made us in the first place?

Who but God could have written the history of the world from its creation to its ultimate destruction? Everything about our modern times matches God's description of the final generation, which was to see Israel become a nation and the focal point of the world.

Who but God could have spelled out moral laws that have proven themselves to be absolute truth throughout the ages? Individuals as well as nations have come to ruin when they attempted to defy God's laws.

Who but God could have written with authority on eternal, invisible things—like heaven, hell, angels, and demons?

Who but God could have written a book introducing himself to mankind? Wherever the Bible has been dispersed, people of all walks of life, all ages, all cultures have met the living Creator God.

Who but God could have written a Book through which he would carry on a lifelong personal relationship with billions of people throughout the history of the world?

God says his Book is alive and has the power to speak with specific clarity to anyone who reads and obeys it. I know from experience that this is true.

I'm enclosing a pamphlet that contains more rea-

sons why the Bible must have been written by God. Have a nice day. Write back soon.

Always,
Patsy

May 22

Dear Patsy,

When your thick envelope arrived, I was sure it contained pictures of you. But it was only an interesting pamphlet and letter. Thanks just the same.

However, I still want a picture of you so I don't have to correspond with a faceless person.

Your letter gave me a lot to think about. By the way, why did God make us?

Answer soon.

Sincerely,
Walter

May 30

Dear Walter,

Would you believe that God made us specifically for himself? Unlike all other members of his creation, mankind was made in God's image.

God is an eternal Spirit and a Person with emotions, intellect, and will. We, too, have eternal spirits and are persons with emotions, intellects, and wills.

85

Like God, we are unique individuals who have a free will that allows us to choose our way. Without a will, we would be no more than programmed robots, incapable of emotions or personal thoughts.

God's basic desire is to love and to be loved. So is ours. He made us for himself to love and for us to love him in return. With our wills, we may choose to love him or not.

God enjoys having a meaningful relationship with people and doing exciting things with them. So do we.

He has a specific plan for the fulfillment of our individual lives. If we choose, we can walk with him and let him unfold his plan before us. From the beginning, our lives were meant to be a divine adventure with God.

It's interesting that you should ask for a "face" to correspond with. Perhaps one reason why God came to us as a human being was to provide us with a face to relate to. Jesus is the face of God, through whom we can relate to the invisible God of the universe.

Anyway, enclosed is a snapshot of me taken in Japan.

Wishing you a nice day.

Always,
Patsy

June 11

Dear Patsy,

Thank you for another fascinating letter. And thank you especially for your pretty picture. I framed it and put it on my kitchen table so I could see it when I write to you, when I eat, when I sit, when I pass by . . .

It's June already. When is the last day of school for you? Do you have any plans for summer vacation?

During the first week of July I'll be in San Jose on a short business trip. I'll also visit my brother, Richard, who lives there. I'd be only two hours away from your home, but I regret that I won't have time to see you on this trip.

Thank you again for your lovely picture. Please write soon.

Sincerely,
Walter

July 16

Dear Walter,

I just realized it's been over a month since I last wrote you. Please forgive me for my long silence. I've been fine but extremely busy.

Immediately after a hectic last week of school, former students and friends from Japan began ar-

riving to visit me. I've been sightseeing to many familiar places in California, enjoying them through the eyes of those who have never before seen America.

I thought of you during the first week of July and wondered if you came to San Jose for your business trip. I hope you had a nice visit with your brother.

Wishing you a happy summer.

Always,
Patsy

July 30

Dear Patsy,

I'm relieved to know that all is well with you. I must admit it concerned me when you didn't write.

I've been busy, too. So much has happened to me since I last wrote. My business trip to San Jose was an interview for a new electrical engineering position in a company there.

To make a long story short, I got the job! I'll move to San Jose at the end of August and begin my new job on September 5.

After I get settled I'll drop in to see you and give you my new address. I hope you're happy about my move, too.

Looking forward to seeing you soon.

Sincerely,
Walter

EIGHT

Temptation

When Walter came to hand me his new San Jose address, he asked if he could drop in again someday.

"Sure," I said, presuming that God would permit an occasional visit from an old pen pal.

But soon Walter became a regular weekend visitor in our home. And I began to look forward to seeing him after a long, challenging week with the children at school. Everything seemed under control between us, but somehow I wrestled with an uneasy feeling. *Surely God doesn't mind my having a male friend,* I rationalized. *After all, we're just visiting at home with my family.*

As the months slipped by, I couldn't help but realize that Walter still desired to marry me.

"I'm going to pick you up and take you home with me tonight," he often joked.

"Now that doesn't sound like a proper thing for a pen pal to do," I would joke back, gently pushing him away. But in my heart, I knew we had grown much closer than mere friends.

At times I feared that our lives were slowly but surely merging toward marriage. I would deliberately note the emptiness in his eyes to remind myself how hollow my life would be if I married a man who had no awareness of Jesus. It seemed to serve as a protective wall to keep me from getting emotionally involved with him, and I told myself I still had enough control over the situation.

But one day the fourth grade teacher came to me after school. "Patsy, is everything all right between you and the Lord?" my Christian friend asked with concern in her voice.

"Why do you ask?"

"Well, you seem to lack peace lately."

I hung my head, shocked that I had noticeably drifted so far from God. I finally had to admit to myself that Walter's friendship had somehow become more important to me than my relationship with God. My priorities were backward. No wonder life seemed so confusing and tasteless lately! I decided that when Walter came to visit on Saturday night I would talk with him about seeing him less often from then on.

Saturday afternoon I entered the kitchen and saw my mother and grandmother engrossed in a discussion at the table.

As I poured myself a tall glass of milk I overheard Obaa-chan, my grandmother, say in Japanese, "Do you think the Sugiyamas should be invited?"

"Definitely. They've always invited us to their important functions," Mom answered in Japanese, writing their name on a list.

"Invite them to what?" I asked, unable to contain my curiosity.

"Oh, we were just wondering who should be invited to the wedding, if and when you and Walter get married," Mom replied sheepishly.

"Who said we're getting married?"

"Well, you two might as well get married," Delphine remarked, flipping through a magazine in the family room. "Whenever I come home, you're sitting around watching TV like an old married couple."

"Yeah. I'm beginning to think he's part of the family already," Diane added, munching on a cookie.

"Well, we're not going to get married. We're just friends," I declared and sat down at the table with my milk.

My grandmother looked gently at me from

across the table. "Pachi," she said, in broken English, mispronouncing my name, "Obaa-chan sinks-so Watta nice-su boy."

"Yes, Obaa-chan, Watta is a nice-su boy, but I don't want to marry him," I said, wondering why I, too, used broken English whenever I spoke to her.

Dad looked up from his newspaper. "If you're not going to marry him, don't lead him on," he said and buried his head in the paper again. No one said any more.

That evening Walter and I watched TV with the family until they all retired to bed. When we were alone, he turned to me and smiled. "How was your week?"

I had planned to ease into the discussion, but since he asked, I admitted, "Not so good. I've been thinking we can't go on seeing each other like this."

"Oh, I've been thinking the same thing."

"You have?"

"Yes. Let's elope to Reno tonight," he joked. But his eyes showed me he wasn't joking altogether.

"I'm serious, Walter! Our futures are at stake here. We're getting older! And since we're not going to marry each other, we need to start meeting other people. Are you trying to meet other girls?"

He put his hands on my arms and looked into my eyes. "Can't you understand that I don't care to meet other girls? I love *you*, Patsy! I don't want to marry anyone else."

"But I told you from the beginning I can't marry you. How long will we go on like this?"

"Until I see you married to someone else, please let me keep hoping that one day you will be my wife," he answered, his eyes filled with tears.

In spite of myself, I embraced him and wept at his hopeless dream and our futile relationship.

That night I tossed and turned in bed, unable to fall asleep. Frustrated, I switched on the light and opened my Bible to search for a word from God to comfort me. My eyes fell on a passage underlined in red—a passage that had often encouraged me to keep waiting for God to bring the right husband to me: "For ye have need of patience, that, after ye have done the will of God, ye might receive the promise. For yet a little while, and he that shall come will come, and will not tarry."*

In the past, I had focused only on the fact that God's promises would come true without tarrying beyond his appointed time. But tonight, the phrase "after ye have done the will of God," seemed to point a convicting finger at me.

"Lord, what must I do to accomplish your will?"

*Hebrews 10:36-37, KJV

Even while I asked, I already knew that God wanted me to relinquish this non-Christian relationship with Walter altogether.

"But . . . but Walter is my only social life! What would I do without his visits . . . without his letters . . . without his friendship?" Loneliness crept into my heart.

Unwilling to let go yet, I shut off the light and cried softly into my pillow. In the stillness of the night, I began to feel a gentle tug at my heart. *Patsy, what about us? What about us? What about us?* I knew it was Jesus.

The tugging soon became an aching passion that throbbed from the depths of my being. *Patsy, I love you. I love you with an everlasting love . . . what about us?*

I broke into sobbing. "Oh, Jesus! I'm so sorry! I love you, too! And I won't let Walter come between us any more!"

I turned on the light, put on my robe, and sat at my desk. Tears streaming down my face, I wrote my farewell letter to Walter:

January 19

Dear Walter,

With this letter, I break all ties with you. I can't go on in the futility of our relationship. And I can't bear to let you hope for a marriage that will never be.

Please accept my deepest gratitude for your friendship and your kindness to me and to my family.

Tonight as I write this final letter, my heart is heavy with something I must tell you before we part. One future day, each of us will pass from this world. The Bible says we are born once, die once, and then face the judgment. After the judgment, each of us will end up in eternal heaven or hell. None of us is sinless and none of us can pass the judgment to enter into a pure, sinless heaven.

But God loved us so much that he was not willing that any of us should perish. That's why he sent his Son, Jesus, to take our sins upon himself, to be judged "guilty" in our stead, and to suffer the death penalty for us. If we put our trust in Jesus and welcome him into our lives for what he has done for us, then when we come before the eternal judgment stand God will declare us "not guilty" because the penalty for our sins has already been paid in full.

No one needs to wonder where he will end up after he dies. In the Bible, God gives us his words on the matter: "And this is the testimony, that God gave us eternal life, and this life is in his Son. He who has the Son has life; he who has not the Son of God has not life. I write this to you who believe in

the name of the Son of God, that you may know
that you have eternal life" (1 John 5:11-13, RSV).

Walter, more than anything else I wish you
would receive God's free gift of eternal life.

Good-bye, precious friend. I'll be praying for
you.

Always,
Patsy

The next day, when I dropped the letter into the mailbox, I felt released from the guilt that had over-shadowed my life for the past four months.

In the weeks that followed, however, I found my-self checking the mail every day for a response from Walter. Then one Saturday a small package arrived from him. I snatched it and ran to my spot behind the tractor shed. Sitting on a crate, I tore open the package. My picture and the pamphlets I had given him tumbled to the ground. I picked them up and searched between the pages for a letter . . . even a note. Nothing! But Walter's unwritten message was clear to me—he would not write nor see me any more.

This was what I had asked for. Then why was I feeling as if my heart would break? Tears blurred my vision as I stared at the winter-dead orchard be-fore me.

At last, I forced myself to turn my eyes upward.

Brushing away the tears, I said, "Lord, I want you to know that I trust you, even when I see no sign of spring ahead."

Deliberately, I began to close Walter out of my heart, and a part of me seemed to die.

"Jesus, you didn't say my life with you would be easy, but you did promise to never leave me nor forsake me . . . and that will be enough for me . . . even if you choose not to have me marry at all."

A feeling of complete peace consumed and warmed my heart. God's unseen hand seemed to take hold of mine, and we walked back to the house together.

NINE

Specifics

Without Walter, I had more time to talk with Jesus. One evening, God seemed to impress on my heart the thought that I should be more specific when I asked him for a husband.

"What do you mean, Lord? Isn't my request for a nice, Christian, Japanese-American man specific enough?" I asked.

Many men could fit that description, he pointed out. *How would you be able to recognize the right one, even if I sent him to you?*

That night I decided to write a list of specifics, just to prove to myself that I knew what I wanted in a husband. I took out a clean sheet of paper and wrote at the top *My Future Husband.* Then I began to compile my list.

1. *Christian*
2. *Japanese-American*
3. *Kind-hearted*
4.

"Number four," I said aloud to myself. "Let me think . . ."

What kind of Christian do you want? Lukewarm or committed? God coached me from within.

Committed Christian, I wrote beside number four. "And I don't want to marry him until you give me a clear word from the Bible, like you did when you took me to Japan," I said as I wrote

5. *Confirmed by God's Word.*

"Oh, and I want you to fill our hearts with your peace, to assure us that you chose us for each other." *Peace,* I wrote next to number six.

How tall do you want him to be? God probed my heart for more details.

"Between three and six inches taller than I am."

How old?

"Oh, between two and six years older than I am," I said as I continued to write.

Any specific personal tastes?

"Well, it would be nice if he enjoyed Japanese food as much as I do. I wouldn't want him to sit at the table and gag every time we had my favorite raw fish for dinner."

How about dislikes?

"Now, Lord, you may think this is silly. But I don't want to have a long last name. Some Japanese names have more than ten letters. I want my new last name to be much shorter than my maiden name." I added that next to number ten.

Don't forget that I promised to bring him to your door, he reminded.

"Oh, yes!" I said, jotting it down.

Anything else? he inquired.

"Not that I can think of right now. But I've wondered what became of the man you had me pray for in Japan. Remember when you woke me up in the middle of the night to pray for my future husband, who you said was in danger of death? From the incredible peace that came into my heart after I prayed, I assume you spared his life."

Miraculously escaped death, I wrote next to number twelve.

Unable to think of more specifics, I folded the list and carefully hid it in a box full of books in my closet, where no one would accidently stumble across it and laugh.

The months slipped by peacefully—February, March, April, May, June—summer vacation again. Without the inner conflict of seeing someone God didn't want me to see, I enjoyed harmony and contentment in my world with him.

Then one evening in early July I received an un-expected phone call that jolted my peaceful world.

"Hello, Patsy. How are you these days?" It was Walter.

"Uh, fine, thank you," I said. "How are you?"

"I'm fine, too."

An awkward silence followed.

Finally, he said, "Do you mind if I ask if you've met someone to marry?"

I cringed at the thought of having Walter come back to intrude on my relationship with God.

"No . . . no, I haven't," I admitted. "Have you?"

"No, I haven't, either."

I remained quiet, not wanting to encourage him to see me again. At last he spoke. "Patsy, I've been thinking seriously about your God, and I've come up with a few questions that I need answered. You're the only Christian I've known closely. Will you write and answer some questions for me?"

My heart sank. *Lord, I don't want to start a pen-pal relationship with him again! What do you want me to say?* I groaned inside.

"I don't know if I can answer your questions, but I'll try," I heard myself reply, in spite of my feelings.

TEN

One and Only

July 7

Dear Patsy,

Thank you for agreeing to write to me again.

You always told me that a good God created us and loves us. But I find that hard to believe when I watch the news on TV and see people suffer from famines, wars, earthquakes, crimes, and diseases.

Why is this world so imperfect? Why doesn't God do something to help us? Can you give me an answer?

Sincerely,
Walter

July 12

Dear Walter,

I, too, would be puzzled about the horrible conditions in the world—if the Bible didn't explain why these things occur.

Of course, our human minds can't comprehend all the ways of the Sovereign God of the universe, but we can know a few basic facts about how the world came to be in its present state.

In the beginning, God created a perfect world. And in it he placed Adam, whom he created in his own image.

God loved Adam so much that he not only placed him on this perfect earth but gave him control and dominion over it.

But Adam and his wife, Eve, turned against their Father God by yielding to Satan's lie and joining him in rebellion. Through this act of rebellion, Adam and the human race became estranged from God. Dominion of the earth passed into Satan's hands.

Using the power to rule inherited from Adam, working primarily in our minds, Satan tries to undermine God and destroy his creation. The Bible calls Satan the father of all lies, a murderer from the beginning, and a thief who comes to steal, kill, and destroy.

He fills the world with perverted philosophies— causing broken lives, broken homes, disease, disaster, and war.

Even in the religious field, Satan sets up innumerable counterfeit religions to confuse sincere seekers from finding God. He misleads people with mock religious experiences and feelings that have no foundation.

But God still longs after his created children who because of disobedience have been taken hostage by Satan. In love, God gave his only begotten Son, Jesus, to die as a ransom to deliver us from Satan's control. He also gave us his written truth, the Bible, by which we can detect the subtle lies of this deceitful "angel of light."

However, a ransom is of no effect unless we choose to accept the freedom it provides. Written truth is of no personal value unless we read and accept it, rejecting the lies it exposes. If we choose, we can belong to God and know truth in a world that's filled with falsehood.

When Jesus came as a baby in Bethlehem, he entered Satan's earthly kingdom. When he died on the cross for our sins, he broke Satan's hold on us. At a future date, he will come again and completely destroy Satan and his dominion over the earth—for Jesus alone is the sovereign King of all creation.

I'm sorry this letter got so long. I hope it answers some of your questions.

Always,
Patsy

July 20

Dear Patsy,

Thank you for your interesting letter.

I've always felt that evil spirits existed—mainly because of the occult, voodoo, and other supernatural black magic around. But I never heard that the Devil ruled the earth and the people on it. If that were true, it would certainly explain why this world suffers from so much evil and disorder.

In your letter you mentioned counterfeit religions. How can a person tell which religions are true and which are the Devil's counterfeits?

Looking forward to hearing your response.

Sincerely,
Walter

August 1

Dear Walter,

I think you will agree that a religion is only as valid as the life of its founder.

During the years when my faith in Jesus was tested, I did some research on the founders of the great religions of the world. Here are some facts I discovered:

No religious leader but Jesus claimed to be God.

No religious leader but Jesus claimed to be the Creator of the universe.

No religious leader but Jesus fulfilled hundreds of detailed prophecies about his miraculous birth, life, death, and resurrection, foretold by God through his prophets centuries beforehand.

*Jesus' life is the most documented life in history. His coming split history in two—*B.C. *and* A.D.

No religious leader but Jesus lived a perfect, miraculous life. He obeyed God, healed the sick, raised the dead, and set men free from satanic oppression.

No religious leader but Jesus was tried and crucified for refusing to deny that he was God. Moreover, he proved himself to be God by bodily rising from the grave after being dead for three days.

No religious leader but Jesus promised to likewise raise you from the dead and make you a home in his heaven if you believe in him.

No religious leader but Jesus returned to heaven before many witnesses.

No other religious leader but Jesus has had countless thousands of followers who chose to be killed rather than deny the reality of Jesus as God. Throughout history Christians have been stoned, hung on crosses, fed to lions, burned at stakes, persecuted, and disowned for their faith in Jesus, which was more precious to them than life itself.

No other religious leader has the witness of God

himself, who declares that his Son Jesus is the only way to God and to heaven.

Walter, only Jesus knows you by name and loves you so much that he laid down his life for you. Only Jesus can show you his nail-pierced hands and feet that bled to pay for your sins and for your deliverance from Satan.

Among the founders of the great religions of the world, only Jesus still lives to talk and walk with you. But don't take just my word for it. Jesus himself tells you to call on him, and he promises to answer. Why don't you call on him and find out for yourself?

Always,
Patsy

August 10

Dear Patsy,

Our letters have been so businesslike that I've neglected to ask about your personal welfare. How have you been? Are you enjoying your summer vacation?

I appreciated your informative letter. I must admit I wasn't aware that Jesus was unique among all the other religious leaders.

I'm becoming interested in making Christianity my religion. Is it best to attend a Christian church and study the doctrine before joining? What do you recommend?

Please write soon.

Sincerely,
Walter

August 21

Dear Walter,

Thank you for inquiring about me. I'm fine and enjoying a restful summer vacation. How are you?

I'm happy to know that you're thinking about becoming a Christian. However, it's important that you clearly understand that Christianity isn't a religion—but a relationship that begins the moment you meet God through Jesus Christ.

A person can't become a Christian by joining a Christian church, nor by believing the doctrine, nor even by following the Bible to the letter.

The Bible says even demons believe Jesus is the Son of God, and tremble, but they certainly aren't Christians. The religious leaders of Jesus' day followed God's laws in detail, but they weren't Christians—because they rejected Jesus. You see, Christianity isn't so much a doctrine to believe, as it is a Person to receive.

No great knowledge of Christian theology is necessary. Even a child can receive Jesus. Remember, I was only eight years old when I became a Christian.

Once you realize that Jesus is the Son of God who died for your sins, all you have to do is receive him as your personal Savior and make him the Lord of your life. Then God performs the miracle of placing in you a new spirit, the Holy Spirit. Through him, you can communicate with God. And your life with God begins.

God promises in the Bible that to as many as receive his Son, Jesus, he will give the power to become the children of God (John 1:12).

Attending a Christian church to learn doctrine is fine. But until you take the step of receiving the living Savior into your life, church-going can never be more than a dead ritual to you.

Always,
Patsy

September 2

Dear Patsy,

I've been fine, too. At work, I'm busy on an important government project. On weekends, more often than not I pass through Lodi on the way to visit my mother in Sacramento.

I guess the engineer in me needs to have a technical explanation for everything—even things about

God. Could you explain to me in more technical terms what you mean by "receiving Jesus?" How can a person receive another person into his life?

Before I close this letter I would like to ask one more question. Would you mind if I attend church with you in Lodi?

Please answer soon.

Sincerely,
Walter

September 12

Dear Walter,

All week, I pondered on how to explain "receiving Jesus" in technical terms to a design engineer. Then I remembered that God designed the marriage relationship to be patterned after Jesus' relationship to the Christian.

Both receiving a spouse and receiving Jesus are acts of personal choice and commitment. Both are consummated by God through a miracle of spiritual union.

A man and a woman receive each other in marriage when they choose each other and make a legal vow to love, honor, and cherish one another—forsaking all others and being faithful only to each other.

A person receives Jesus into his life when he asks

111

him to be his personal Savior and Lord and vows to love, honor, and obey him—forsaking Satan and sin, and being faithful only to Jesus.

I hope this simple explanation is technical enough for you.

Regarding church, you're welcome to attend with me if you wish. Sunday school starts at 9:30, worship service at 10:45. If you come to my home at nine o'clock, we should get there in plenty of time.

Always,
Patsy

ELEVEN

Test of Obedience

The moment I read Walter's letter asking if he could attend church with me, it occurred to me that if he became a Christian, God might ask me to marry him. I was delighted that Walter might soon meet Jesus, but I felt inexplicably disappointed over the thought of marrying him.

I walked out beyond the tractor shed to the walnut orchard to sort out my mixed emotions. A fruitful crop of walnuts almost ready for harvest loaded the branches. Some of the leaves had already turned yellow and had dropped to the ground.

I trudged along over dry dirt clods, mumbling to myself. "Why don't I want to marry Walter? He's nice. But I'm sure I could live without him." That was my problem. Someone had once advised me to marry a person not merely because I felt I could live with him, but because I felt I couldn't live without

him. I wondered if my feelings would change when
I saw him again.

However, to my dismay, when Walter came I was
almost bored being with him. To make matters
worse, he still seemed interested in me, and every
Sunday he seemed to be getting closer to becoming
a Christian.

Anxiety mounted in my heart. "Please, God,
don't ask me to marry Walter!" I begged.

On the fourth Sunday Walter attended church
with me, God's still, small voice confronted my
heart with the question I dreaded to hear: *Patsy, if
Walter becomes a Christian, will you marry him?* I
glanced at Walter sitting beside me in the pew.
Somehow my feelings for him seemed as detached
and dead as the dried leaves under the walnut trees.
But, Lord, I don't love him! my heart cried in
protest.

After church, Walter said he needed to prepare
for a business trip and couldn't come next Sunday.
I felt relieved to have two weeks away from him to
think.

However, every time I contemplated marriage to
him, an impenetrable wall of deadness blocked all
anticipation of a happy future with him. How could
God ask me to marry someone I was not attracted
to, when I had waited thirty years to marry the man
of his choice?

Patsy, you always said I could choose your husband for you, God reminded me. *Have you changed your mind?*

"No, Lord, I haven't changed my mind, but I assumed you would choose someone that I at least liked a lot," I responded icily.

That next Sunday I went alone to church. My willful heart received nothing from the sermon. When church was dismissed, I wove quickly through the crowd toward the exit.

Suddenly, I bumped into a woman who had been a missionary in Trinidad.

"Oh, Patsy, darling, how are you today?" she asked.

"Fine, thank you. How are you?" I said, trying not to sound too impatient.

"Where is your nice gentleman friend today?" she asked leisurely.

"He's getting ready for a business trip and couldn't come."

Then an idea occurred to me. *I should ask her about my dilemma. She's walked with God for a long time. She ought to know.*

"May I ask you a question?" I said hesitantly.

"Sure, darling. What is it?" she responded sweetly.

"Well, do you think God makes a person do what she or he definitely doesn't want to do?"

"God doesn't *make* us do anything we don't choose to do. He tells us what he wants us to do, then allows us to decide whether or not to trust his judgment," she explained.

"I see." I felt dissatisfied with her general answer to my general question.

"How about in the case of marriage? Would God ask a person to marry someone he or she doesn't have any feelings for?" I tried my evasive approach again.

"Oh, are you referring to the nice young gentleman who comes to church with you?" she asked, perceiving the real question through my cover.

"Yes," I admitted.

"Well, darling, sometimes God works in mysterious ways, and we have to trust him in the parts we don't understand," she said with a twinkle in her eyes.

Something about the way she smiled made me feel that she sided with God on this issue about Walter. I regretted having asked her about it.

By Thursday, I had asked several more Christians if they thought God forced people to marry someone they didn't love.

"Oh no!" they all responded—mostly because of the way I worded the question. But even their votes of confidence didn't ease the unsettled feeling inside of me.

By Friday night I was overcome by self-imposed misery. I threw myself on the bed and wept bitterly.

Why are you fighting your God, who loves you? He wants to give you only what's best for you, I told myself. I cried out my frustrations until I lay limply on the bed, drained of emotion. In the stillness of my room I sensed God waiting to talk with me. Finally, I sat up and spoke to him quietly.

"Heavenly Father, please forgive me for acting like a selfish, spoiled child. . . . I'm sorry for treating you so badly during these past few weeks."

God's sweet forgiveness flowed into my heart, but I knew unfinished business still separated us.

"Lord, I really do want to trust you to choose my husband for me," I said, longing for his peace to return to my heart.

You can trust me, my child. You can, if you choose. God seemed to cheer me on.

Slowly, deliberately, I opened my hands palms up and lifted them above my head. Looking up with tear-filled eyes, I said, "Heavenly Father, I will trust you to marry me to anyone you choose for me . . . even someone I don't love."

Even Walter?

"Yes . . . even Walter."

Peace poured into my heart like pure water over parched land. However, my feelings toward Walter remained lifeless.

That Saturday night Walter came and asked another question about Christianity. After he left I felt discouraged. He seemed to be making such slow progress toward God. *I've been answering his questions about God for two years!* I thought. *Maybe he's one of those who forever learns but never receives.*

On Sunday Walter attended church with me. After the minister prayed the benedictory prayer he looked across the congregation and added, "I feel that God is telling me that someone here wants to invite Jesus into his life today. If you felt a yearning for God during the service I would say that Jesus is knocking on your heart's door, drawing you to himself.

"The congregation is dismissed, but I will remain at the altar to pray with anyone who wants to receive Jesus as Savior and Lord this morning."

The people shuffled toward the door. I turned to leave, but Walter tapped me on the shoulder. "Patsy, will you wait for me here? I'm going to have the minister pray with me."

My mouth dropped open, and I watched in unbelief as Walter walked down the long aisle toward the minister.

Close friends rushed over to me excitedly. We knelt in the pews and thanked God and wept for joy. When we arose from our knees, I saw the minister shake Walter's hand. Then abruptly, something deep in my heart began to rumble, like the beginning of an earthquake. The shaking grew stronger and more violent as Walter came up the aisle toward me. Suddenly, with an almost audible crash, the impenetrable wall between us cracked, shattered, and crumbled to the ground.

Walter stood before me, and I saw him as if for the first time. I searched his eyes. The deadness that had always been there had already been replaced by his newborn life from God.

"Congratulations!" I said, amazed that once again it seemed so natural to hug him. I stepped aside for the others to congratulate him, too, but I couldn't take my eyes off of him.

Dear Jesus, my heart whispered. *What is this feeling that draws me to Walter now? . . . Am I falling in love with him?*

TWELVE

The Surprise

During the month after Walter met Jesus our mutual love for God became the foundation for a new kind of friendship between us. Sometimes after church he stayed for lunch and visited before going home. I loved to be near him, and God seemed to be knitting our hearts together. But Walter never mentioned that he loved me any more.

One Sunday afternoon in early December we walked around the yard until we came to my special spot behind the tractor shed. Walter offered me a crate to sit on and pulled up another beside me.

I felt he had something to say, but we just sat quietly looking across the late autumn countryside—rustic and serene. A carpet of brown leaves covered the ground under each walnut tree. Beyond the wire fence the neighbor's alfalfa had been harvested and neatly stacked in bales.

After a long while, I asked, "What are you thinking?"

"I'm thinking how much I love you and how much I still want to marry you." He turned to me and took my hand.

Tears sprang to my eyes. "I love you, too, Walter," I said, revealing what my heart had longed to tell him for the past month.

"You do?" He gathered me into his arms. "Then will you marry me?" he whispered into my ear.

"I want to say yes, but I can't just yet." I sighed, gently pushing away from him.

"Why?"

"Because I'm not comfortable making big decisions on mere feelings. I need time to ask God, so I can be sure that this is what he wants for us. . . . And I have a marriage list I wrote with God. I want to check that, too." I stood up.

"How long will that take?" he asked, standing beside me.

"I don't know. Remember when I went to Japan? It took six months before God spoke to me through the Bible and told me he definitely wanted me to go and teach there." I sat back down on the crate.

"How can the Bible tell you to go to Japan?" Walter asked, seating himself next to me again.

"Well, it's a miracle God does through his Holy Spirit, who lives inside our hearts. He brings words in the Bible to life and personalizes them to our specific situation."

"Really? But how can a person know which words are God's answers to his particular circumstances?"

"I don't know how to explain it, but somehow you'll know that God is talking directly to you when you read a certain passage."

"But how do you know? Is it like a clear understanding in your head?"

I pondered Walter's difficult question. "No, it's more than that. It's like something solid in your heart that can't be moved. And God's peace confirms that it's really from him."

Walter became pensive, then spoke quietly. "I think I'll read the Bible and try to get an answer about our marriage, too."

"You will?" I jumped up, hardly able to believe what I heard. My mind raced wildly. "You know what would be exciting to do?" I exclaimed. "Let's ask God to speak to us through the same verse, if he wants us to marry each other!"

Walter hesitated. "Well . . . OK."

That evening he left early, looking discouraged.

On Monday night I decided to do some casual reading in my *Living Bible,* presuming it would take months before God would speak to me about marriage.

I lay in bed on my stomach and bowed my head to pray before I began to read. "Lord, I'm almost certain you want me to marry Walter, but I ask you to give me a specific verse that can be laid as a foundation for our marriage. Please tell me clearly if I'm to marry Walter."

I propped myself up on one elbow, opened the Bible to its marker in First Thessalonians, chapter two, and continued to read there. Suddenly, a short exclamation in verse nineteen seemed to leap off the page into my heart: "It is you!"

I blinked in surprise and read the whole verse aloud: "It is you! Yes, you will bring us much joy as we stand together before our Lord Jesus Christ when he comes back again."

The verse gripped my heart.

"Father, God! Are you telling me it *is* Walter?"

A calm, unshakable certainty filled my being. I knew that God had chosen Walter for me. I wanted to shout for joy! But not wishing my family to think I'd gone insane, I quietly celebrated with God in my bedroom.

The next morning before school began I shared my excitement with two fellow teachers who listened with dancing eyes.

"Now all I have to do is wait for Walter to get the same verse from God," I concluded.

"Patsy, that's wonderful! But are you sure God

wants to speak to Walter through the same verse? If he doesn't, you may be in for a long wait," the fourth-grade teacher lovingly advised.

"That's right!" the vivacious, young, second-grade teacher exclaimed, her imagination tickled. "I can see it now—Walter, eighty years old, coming with a tattered Bible in his hand."

She bent over and hobbled toward me, pretending to have a cane in one hand and a Bible in the other. In a cracking voice, she said, "Pa-atsy, is this the ri-ight verse?"

Then she pretended to be a nearsighted old lady who checked the verse with a magnifying glass held in her shaky hand. "N-no, Walter, go b-back and g-guess again!"

We all burst into laughter. But I began to worry that perhaps I had imposed one of my whims on God.

That evening when Walter phoned I told him God had spoken to me through a verse. I couldn't resist adding that I found the verse in Thessalonians.

"That's nice," he said, sounding bewildered. "I'll read that section."

"I'll pray for you," I said, trying to encourage him, but I had a depressed feeling that I would need to wait a long, long time.

However, Walter surprised me with a phone call

on Friday night. "I think God gave me his answer about us," he said.

"He did?" I exclaimed, nearly dropping the phone. "How do you know?"

"Well, as I read along, these particular verses caught my attention. And as I tried to read on I felt impressed to reread the same verses. When I did, a peaceful feeling came over me and I knew that God was pointing to them for us. Would you like to know what the verses are?"

"Yes, I would," I said, my heart pounding.

"One Thessalonians, chapter three, verses twelve and thirteen."

"Oh, . . . they're not the same as mine, but that's OK," I said, trying to hide my disappointment. "I don't have my Bible by the phone. Would you read it to me?" I slumped in the kitchen chair, discouraged, but willing to listen.

"It says, 'And may the Lord make your love to grow and overflow to each other and to everyone else, just as our love does toward you. This will result in your hearts being made strong, sinless and holy by God our Father, so that you may stand before him guiltless on that day when our Lord Jesus Christ returns with all those who belong to him.' "

An unexpected sense of peace filled me as Walter read the verses God had given him, and I sat up straighter in the chair. My heart stirred with the understanding that while God had not given us the same reference, he had given us the same message. He had told us both that we would love and serve him and stand together before our Lord Jesus when he returned to earth.

"Those are beautiful verses. They speak to me, too," I stated cautiously, my head spinning from the sudden turn of events.

"Patsy, I have to work tomorrow, but I'll drop in to see you on the way back to Sacramento if it's not too late," he said.

The next morning a letter arrived from a missionary friend of mine in Japan. I had written her about Walter soon after he became a Christian. Eagerly, I opened her letter and scanned to the part about him:

> *I'm so happy that Walter has become a Christian! He sounds like a very nice man, but may I caution you to make sure he is a committed Christian before you consider marriage to him. An uncommitted Christian is almost worse than a person who doesn't know God at all.*
>
> *Matthew 6:21 says, "For where your treasure is, there will your heart be also" (KJV). Where he invests his money is one outward indicator of where his heart commitments are. Do you know if he's tithing his income? A person who with-*

*holds from God the money that rightfully be-
longs to him is an uncommitted Christian yet.*

I put down the letter and prayed, "Lord, I know I
need to marry a committed Christian, and I've seen
many evidences of Walter's commitment to you." I
looked at the letter as if I had to give an explanation. "Commitment involves a lot more than just
paying tithes. Walter is such a young Christian. He
may not even know that one tenth of his income
belongs to God."

I began to wonder how I could discreetly find out
if he tithed. But I didn't have to wonder long. Later
that evening when Walter came, he had a question
to ask me.

"I've set aside the tithe out of my paycheck this
month. Can you tell me where I should give it?"

"To the church you attend regularly," I answered,
smiling inside at God.

Walter seemed weary from the long week and
late driving. I served him hot tea, and we sat quietly
by the fireplace in the family room.

"Would you care to watch TV?" I asked.

"No, I'm too tired to start watching a long program. Why don't you just tell me about the marriage list you mentioned last weekend. What's on
it?"

"I can't remember exactly. It's a list of specifics I

want in a husband. God helped me write it about eleven months ago. Let me go get it and see how we're doing."

I went to my closet and dug it out of its hiding place under the books. When I returned to the family room, Walter had leaned his head back on the couch and closed his eyes.

"Would you read it to me?" he asked, looking as though he might fall asleep at any minute.

I noticed the first three items already fulfilled and began to check them off as I read.

"One: Christian . . . check. Two: Japanese-American . . . check. Three: Kind-hearted . . . check. Are you listening?" I asked, seeing him stifle a yawn.

"Yes, go on," he replied, shifting to a more comfortable position.

"Four: Committed Christian . . . check." I smiled, remembering his tithe.

"Five: Confirmed by God's Word . . . check." I was still amazed at the fast miracle God had performed. "Six: Peace . . . check. Seven: Between three and six inches taller. . . . How tall are you, Walter?"

"Five feet, five inches."

"I'm five feet, exactly."

"Check," he said with a smile.

"Eight: Between two and six years older."

"Check," he said.

"Nine: Likes Japanese food," I read.

"Double check," Walter answered, seeming to lose his weariness.

"Ten: Short last name." I smiled as I thought of Walter's last name, Oda.

"Check," he said. "If it were much shorter, people would mistake it for initials!"

We laughed.

"Eleven: Brought to my door . . . check," I said, tears filling my eyes as I recalled how many times I had tried to get rid of Walter and how many times God had brought him back to my door.

"Twelve: Miraculously escaped death," I read.

Walter suddenly sat straight up, wide awake. "What made you put that down?"

Startled, I stammered, "Well . . . uh . . . two years ago in May, just before I came home from Japan, I woke up in the middle of the night feeling certain that the man God meant for me to marry was in danger of being killed. And I knew if I didn't pray for him, he would die."

Walter's eyes grew big as he listened.

"My heart became heavy for this man, and I prayed into the night until my burden for his life lifted. Then peace came and I fell back to sleep."

Walter stared at me, speechless.

"Why are you looking at me like that?" I asked.

"Two years ago in June, I was almost killed in a car accident." Walter spoke in a daze. "The inside of the car was soaked with my blood. People who saw my car afterward said no person could have lived through it."

He turned to me. "Patsy . . . I was the man you prayed for in Japan!"

The room seemed filled with the presence of God, and we sat in silent awe.

After a long while, almost reverently, I picked up the list. But when I looked at it, every item had been checked. I turned the paper over and looked on the other side. Nothing more.

"Walter," I heard myself whisper, "I think we're engaged!"

Speechless, we stared at the checked list, then at each other. Wondrous peace overwhelmed me. When my eyes met Walter's I knew he, too, had experienced God's incredible confirmation in his heart.

The next day we received our parents' blessings on our decision to marry, and we joyously announced our engagement to our "matchmakers," relatives, and friends.

During the next eight months that led to our wedding day, God continued to enrich our love with his love and enhance our joy with his surprises along the way.

One surprise came just in time to be printed in our wedding program. While I slept in the midnight hours, I became conscious of a rhythmic phrase that seemed to pulsate from deep within me. It was beautiful, and I didn't want to lose it. Groggily, I turned on the light and scribbled the words on a tablet. Then more phrases emerged. I continued to write until they stopped.

The next morning when I read my sleepy handwriting I discovered a poem for Walter—a wedding sonnet, metered and rhymed:

With solemn, sacred vows to thee I wed
And set my heart to love and honor thee
Through all the seasons of our life ahead,
For thee alone were made by God for me.

Though knowing thee in part—still strangers we,
With joy I trust my life into thy care.
From this day forth to walk thru life with thee,
To dream, to work, discover and to share.

For richer or for poorer, sun or rain,
May peace and true contentment be our stay.
In sickness and in health, in loss or gain,
With strength and purpose may we live each day.

And when our journey here on earth is through,
May by God's grace, our love be found still true.

At last our August wedding day arrived. Hundreds of friends and relatives gathered in the church where Walter had received Jesus ten months before.

The candles were lit, the singers performed, and the bridesmaids and groomsmen moved to their places. The minister nodded to the organist and pianist to begin the bridal march.

The train on my ivory-laced gown flowed behind me as I walked down the long aisle with Dad. I noticed my childhood Sunday school teacher, Joanne, and her mother, Mrs. Smith, seated among the guests. From the time I had become of marriageable age, they had prayed that God would give me a Christian husband. Today they had traveled from a distant city to celebrate God's answer to their prayers.

At the altar, Walter took my hand. We stood and faced each other while the soloist began a new song. Through my delicate veil, I gazed into Walter's eyes and wondered at the glow of the life of Jesus in him.

Finally, it was time for us to repeat our vows after the minister and receive each other in marriage. For a moment, my heart sped back to that day so long ago when, as a child, I had repeated a prayer after Joanne and received Jesus as my Savior and Lord.

Now with that same certainty in my heart, I

looked into Walter's eyes and repeated my vows.

"I, Patsy, take you, Walter, to be my wedded husband. To love, honor, and cherish you—forsaking all others, to be faithful to you only, as long as we both shall live."

Epilogue

When the editor of this book asked me to write a short summary of our life together after the wedding, I asked Walter how he would write it.

"And they lived happily ever after," he quickly replied, smiling.

I smiled back, delighting in his answer, knowing that our thirteen years of marriage have been truly happy ones. Inwardly I smiled at God, who had helped us through the normal struggles and adjustments of married life.

Since our wedding, Walter and I have lived in San Jose, California, where he still works as an electrical engineer. We are active members in the San Jose Open Bible Church, where we have steadily grown more in love with Jesus. We have continually enjoyed the fellowship of wonderful Christians who love God, too.

I have not taught in the public schools since I married, but God has opened other areas of teaching for me. Early in my marriage, he gave me the special privilege of teaching children in an after-school Bible class. Walter shared my joy as God allowed me to introduce many children to Jesus in these classes. Although we have no physical children, God has fulfilled our lives with many spiritual children.

Then God unfolded yet another phase of his plan for our lives. Christian friends began coming to our home just to talk about what Jesus was doing in their lives. It was so much fun that friends invited more friends. Soon our get-togethers evolved into an exciting weekly fellowship and Bible study that still meets now, eleven years later.

Over the years, God began to build in our hearts a growing desire to share the knowledge of Jesus through a book. This book, recording the unique courtship he had planned for us, is the result.

As we look back on the various events and activities of our married life, we can see one lovely, unifying theme throughout—Jesus, the living God, whom we love and serve. The better we come to know him, the more we realize that he is the source of love and joy for our marriage, and he is the source of contentment for all our lives.

To order additional copies of

send \$9.99 plus \$3.95 shipping and handling to

Books, Etc.
PO Box 1406
Mukilteo, WA 98275

or have your credit card ready and call

(800) 917-BOOK